D1135211

FISHING
SEASON

R. Mcphail.

FISHING SEASON

An Artist's Fishing Year

Rodger McPhail

Text by
Colin Laurie McKelvie

SWAN·HILL
PRESS

in association with
The Tryon Gallery
ENGLAND

Illustrations © Copyright 1990 Rodger McPhail

Text © Copyright 1990 Colin Laurie McKelvie

First published in 1990 by Swan Hill Press, an imprint of
Airlife Publishing Ltd. in association
with The Tryon Gallery Ltd., London

British Library Cataloguing in Publication Data
McPhail, Rodger, 1953-
    Fishing season
    1. Angling
    I. Title
    799.120941

ISBN 1 85310 145 1

Swan Hill Press

An Imprint of Airlife Publishing Ltd

101 Longden Road, Shrewsbury SY3 9EB, England

Printed in England by
Livesey Ltd., Shrewsbury

INTRODUCTION

The history of fishing with rod and line is very ancient. We look in vain for any precise point at which the sport began, or any particular culture or civilisation to which we can ascribe with certainty its invention and development. All we can say with confidence is that since the dawn of time men have peered into rivers and streams, lakes and the sea itself; they have seen and coveted the fish that swim there; and what probably began as a necessary food gathering operation has since evolved into a pleasurable and wholly absorbing pastime, satisfying for its own sake and a recreation in every sense of that word.

The ancient Greeks and Romans knew all about angling with rod, hook and line, and in particular their writers appear to have attributed the development of fly-fishing to the Macedonians. Archaeological remains from the Stone Age clearly reveal that early man used crude hooks of bone and wood to catch his fish, along with his fish spears and nets. Many of the earliest and most primitive items of fishing tackle have remained virtually unchanged and in common use until recent times, for example among the Inuit peoples of the Arctic regions and the tribes of south-east Asia and the Pacific islands.

At what point in history did rod-and-line fishing cease to be merely a means of food gathering and become a pastime, something worth doing for its own sake? That important change, from necessary subsistence fishing to pleasurable and recreational angling must have come about as a by-product of the gradual development of human societies from hunter-gatherers into more settled communities, husbanding their flocks and herds, growing their annual crops and able to catch ample fish for food using nets and traps. Some cultures even maintained stocks of their favourite species of fish in special ponds and purpose built stews, as an important source of immediately accessible food. Then fishing with rod and line, like falconry and hunting with hounds, ceased to be only a utilitarian and functional means of supplying the table and became a delightful and absorbing end in itself, a self-justifying pastime which for many enthusiastic fishers of every generation has often developed into a consuming passion.

Wherein lies the special attraction and challenge of fishing? Much of its appeal must be purely aesthetic, the simple enjoyment of a peaceful activity in the countryside and often among wonderfully scenic surroundings. There is something calming and revitalising in the very fact of being in close proximity to water, something which poets and mystics and fishermen have always recognised, and which scientists strive to explain in terms of the sense of positive well-being induced by a source of negative ions. 'To refresh the soul by the side of running water' sounds less convincingly scientific, but most fishermen will still intuitively understand what the phrase means.

The successful fisher must also become to some degree a creature of two worlds. Fish are denizens of a different medium and of a wholly different set of environments, by comparison with man who walks on the surface of the earth and breathes the open air. To cast our bait or lure into the water is to make a leap, to seek to establish a direct link which bridges the gulf between our own world and an alien and mysterious milieu. Surely that is why there is an irresistible instinct to stop and peer over bridges, to seek continually for a glimpse of those shadowy torpedo shapes which hang in midwater in the pools and cruise among the fronds of weed. That is part of the reason why we go fishing.

The commercial fisherman with his nets can set about his work in the certain knowledge that if his fish are there, he will catch them. The sporting shot knows that if his quarry is within range and if his aim is true he will account for his grouse or pheasant, his roebuck or his stag. No such certainties exist for him who goes fishing with a rod and line. Even when a feeding fish has been spotted and identified; even when the finest bait or lure or fly has been selected and presented with the utmost care and skill; even when the tackle is the most expensive and the fisher's dextrous skills have been finely tuned by long years of practice — there is still no guarantee that the fish will take or, having taken, that he will be held, played and brought to hand successfully. A salmon may be resting in a known taking lie in a good pool, the fisher may cast his line with consummate artistry and present a proven fly to the fish with all the care and accuracy that one could wish — but nothing he can do will necessarily induce that fish to take his fly. The fish itself is the unknown quantity, the unpredictable and seemingly self-willed element in a complex and infinitely subtle equation. Is it this imponderable element in fishing which makes success so very sweet and satisfying? Is that what drives us back again and again, despite failures and frustration, to try our chances once more?

Picture the dedicated fisherman's tackle room. On the wall is a rack full of fishing rods, each in its labelled bag: above it is a long shelf of reels, each oiled and dully gleaming. Imagine what tales this tackle could tell — of spring salmon fishing, with the big double-handed rod, the heaviest line and the largest fly reel, with ice in the rod rings and grue in the river, and the firm, determined take of a heavy February salmon fresh up from the tide. Beside it there are also lighter, shorter salmon rods for smaller rivers and for the low water conditions of summer, when lighter tackle is the norm and the chief quarry are lively grilse and summer salmon.

The single-handed trout rods and the smaller reels recall days by the streams and on the lochs, casting a nymph or a dry fly upstream over wary chalk stream trout hanging in the current of the pellucid water, or rolling a three-fly cast of wet flies from a gently drifting boat while the air rings with the scolding cries of nesting greenshank and golden plover. One of the reels carries coils of monofilament and a final section of floss blow-line, hinting at days spent dapping both artificial and natural flies during the mayfly season, and later tempting the big stillwater trout with dapped daddy-longlegs and grasshoppers in August and September.

Beside the rods of split cane and carbon fibre hang others of tubular and solid glass, their special fittings proof against the corrosion of salt water: rods for casting a glittering sand eel or a trio of feathered lures into the mackerel-crowded seas of August; rods for fishing deep in the dark depths below the sea-fisher's mark, to take cod and pollock and bass; rods for casting a large and lurid fly to the lightning-fast bonefish and the massive tarpon in the warm shallows off the coast of Central America.

There is a powerful spinning rod for autumn pike, and next to it hang special rods for carp, which recall long and solitary vigils by meres and lakes in the velvety near-darkness from a summer dusk right through to early dawn. Alongside hangs a more delicate wand which could tell many a tale of brisk, crisp early winter days spent trotting a gilt-tail worm or a maggot for grayling, as fallen leaves litter the river's surface and the first frosts rime the rushes and flags along the banks.

There too, no taller than a man and fashioned in a single solid piece, is the big-game rod, with its massive brazen multiplying reel, its roller rings and its clips for stabilisers and a fighting harness. Marlin and sailfish, barracuda and tuna have all bent that rod and strained that braided line in warm ocean waters far away under the heat and glare of a tropical sun.

Rodger McPhail has fished for all these species, under these conditions and with this varied array of tackle. His understanding of each and every one of the fishing scenes he paints has been derived from direct personal experience, and his hand and eye are guided by an unusually acute and accurate visual memory. Anyone who has fished with Rodger, or who has simply enjoyed his company in an outdoor setting, will know with what vivid intensity and concentration he will stop to study the small details of fins and scales, the patterns and texture of trees and plants, and the subtleties of the plumage and coloration of even the most familiar birds. For Rodger there is a great deal more to fishing than the mere catching of fish; there is a total absorption and involvement with the experience in all its facets, allied to an enviable ability to remember the minute details of what he has seen and to recall them in vivid and faithful images on paper and canvas.

SPRING

The complete angler can fish all the year round, for some testing and exciting species of fish are always in season. In that sense our fishing season has no obvious beginning and no particular end. So let us follow the sequence of the seasons, and begin with the turn of the New Year and the first days of early spring.

There is the chill but challenging prospect of fresh, early run salmon in great rivers like Tweed, and covering the wide and spacious waters of a big river often calls for a boat and the skills and advice of an experienced boatman, with the fisherman placed astern in a swivel chair to have maximum command of the water, and of the fish when it is hooked. A capable ghillie can hold the boat steady in the best places, to allow his Rod to cover the known lies and taking spots. But in spring most salmon rivers have their share of kelts too, feeble and gaunt after the stresses of spawning and wearing the characteristically harsh metallic livery of the spent fish, so different from the silvery brightness of a fresh-run salmon. The kelt's vent is swollen, its tail and fins ragged and its gills infested with parasites, and we return it to the water as gently as we can, and wish it well on its way, perhaps to return and spawn again some day in this, the river of its birth.

On the chalk streams of Wessex there are signs of new life stirring in the spring. The streamlined and aerobatic hobbies have returned from south of the Mediterranean to nest again amid water meadows lush with fresh spring grass, and the first damsel flies have appeared. Snipe are making their drumming courtship flights over their nesting sites in the damp meadows and there are fresh-run salmon in the Frome — where even a passing train can add to the other natural hazards where the flyfisher's fly or line may be snagged.

The warmer weather encourages the gradual emergence of countless species of insects, and these in turn are pursued by many newly arrived insectivorous spring migrant birds, including swallows and martins, terns and the insistently calling cuckoo. On the river the coming of mid-May sees the first hatches of mayflies, which rise as nymphs after their two-year development among the sands and gravels of the river bed, and the duns hatch on the water's surface with a gentle flutter of greenish-yellow wings. Hares are more conspicuously active than at other times of the year as they chase and mate on the fields and downs, while predators like the stoat and the owl must hunt extra hard to feed their growing young. To be by the river with a fishing rod is to be drawn into all the sights and sounds of the countryside in spring, to witness the innumerable little incidents of life and death among wild creatures.

These are indeed the 'halcyon days' on the chalk streams, where the halcyon or kingfisher is a bright and shimmering sight, which is both fairly common and perennially thrilling. Swans with their young share the riverside with the turtle doves and the water voles, brown trout hang like shadowy torpedoes in their accustomed lies and grayling prepare for their annual spawning. The mayfly hatch on the Test and other south country chalk streams is one of the highlights of the flyfisher's year, especially when trout can be stalked and caught on dry flies which particularly imitate the emergent insect, or the spent gnat which collapses lifeless on the water after the frenzied aerial mating dance and the laying of the eggs on the water's surface. The fertile eggs sink to the sands and gravel of the river bed, and so the two-year cycle of the mayfly's life begins anew. Of all the limpid chalk streams of southern England the Test has long been queen, and the capital of chalk stream mayfly fishing is the town of Stockbridge, mecca for hundreds of anglers over many generations and headquarters of the Houghton Club. This is the richest and most exclusive of all angling clubs, whose membership is limited to a maximum of twenty-four and whose private waters are some of the most exciting and productive river trout fishing in the world.

Far off in the northern highlands the gorse is now in full bloom as spring enlivens the glens with the sights and sounds of nesting oystercatchers, lark song and the first crop of young lambs. Yet even on a bright spring day the remnants of old cottages and abandoned farm steadings can serve as melancholy reminders of the highland clearances, when the clans were broken and scattered in the aftermath of the Jacobite defeat at Culloden in 1746, and the drift away from the land carried on through the nineteenth century with the eviction of

tenants from their crofts and farms, usually to make way for sheep or deer. Now the glens are the depopulated and lonely haunts of the birds and the otters, the salmon — and the salmon fishers.

These northern glens are the strongholds of some of our rarest birds and mammals. Here are some of the most flourishing local populations of otters, and the merlin, smallest of our native falcons, breeds amid the rolling hills.

The salmon's life in fresh water begins with the growth of the fertilised egg in the security of the redd among the river gravels. The alevin develops, nourished by its yolk sac, and passes through the successive stages of the fry and the parr, with its distinctive thumbprint markings on its flanks. At each stage of its development there are natural enemies, in the form of dippers, lovers of the rough and rocky streams, the predatory kingfishers and the mergansers, goosanders and cormorants with their especial fondness for the parr of salmon. The survivors will reach some six or seven inches in length before secretions of guanine turn them silvery bright and they begin to drop down to the estuary as migrant smolts, having completed the vital but hazardous freshwater stages of their development.

Trout, which enjoy such a privileged position in so many southern waters, are traditionally deemed to be little better than vermin on these northern salmon rivers, and are too often dismissed as unwelcome carnivores which devour the salmon eggs and feast on the fry and parr. Fierce maledictions are also directed at the goosander and the merganser, both sawbilled birds and prominent predators on small fish. Both have enjoyed full legal protection since 1981, but many salmon fisheries proprietors have applied to the Nature Conservancy Council for special licences to keep their numbers in check by shooting.

Spring is spawning time for most species of coarse fish, and also for the grayling, whose adipose fin marks him out as a full member of the salmonid family and a cousin of the trout and the salmon. Pike and chub, sticklebacks and perch pair and deposit their eggs on the mud or sand of the river bottom or among sunken vegetation.

For trout fishermen everywhere late spring is a prime time of the sporting year, and on the Test, that most celebrated of all dry fly trout streams, a cautious flyfisher takes endless pains to disentangle his fly from a bankside snag without disturbing the feeding fish he has marked down. In Wales, too, the trout flyfisher casts his tiny, soft hackled flies to the waiting trout, while the sky is full of the dipping, swirling flights of swallows and martins and the bleating calls of young lambs.

Afloat on a heaving swell and riding at anchor on a mark off the shoreline cliffs, the sea fisher tries for cod and pollock, or struggles to disentangle a birdsnest chaos of monofilament line on his multiplying reel, while wooden-winged fulmars circle and swirl and eider ducks ride at ease on the swell. The fulmar with its curiously stiff-winged flight and its churring, resonant call has become much more numerous around British coasts in recent times, and its only disagreeable characteristic is its tendency to regurgitate a stream of foul and fishy smelling oil if it is disturbed or frightened. Puffins have no such objectionable tendencies, but have an engagingly comic appearance, especially when their heavy and richly coloured bills are crammed and draped with small fish for their hungry young. Small and round-bodied, these little 'sea parrots' have the swift, blurr-winged flight which is characteristic of the auk family.

The warmer weather and longer hours of daylight are ideal conditions in which to introduce young children to their first taste of fishing, perhaps with a small net, a short rod or just a stick with a length of line and a hook. There is infinite pleasure for them in the small events of a few hours by the river or among the rock pools along the shore, and the jamjars are carried proudly home full of tadpoles, minnows and sticklebacks.

In the valley of the Findhorn in Morayshire the sights and sounds of late spring include the nesting red grouse, ospreys fishing with spectacular verve and skill to feed their growing young, and small family parties of roe deer in their summer coats of foxy red, preparing for the coming rutting time in late July. The cock grouse have secured their breeding territories and each has found a mate, and they hold and defend both against the intrusion of other males with short-tempered aggression. A favourite habit is for the cock grouse to stand atop a mound or small knoll, to give him a commanding view and to enable him to proclaim his presence by sight and sound to nearby would-be rivals and intruders. The chuckling calls of cock grouse towards dusk are characteristic of the heather uplands in spring.

Ospreys have returned in increasing numbers to Scotland, ever since the first breeding pair returned from Europe and took up their well publicised residence on Speyside in the 1960s. By the late 1980s an estimated eighty pairs of ospreys were breeding in the central highlands, and the rocky valley of the Findhorn, with its gorges and its stands of mature Scots pine, is one of their regular haunts. There is a special affinity between the game fisherman and the osprey, each an expert fisher in his own way.

BLACK CLO

GLASS

MIRRO

R. McPhail

SUMMER

During the long hours of daylight in high summer the coarse fisher, the salmon enthusiast and the sea angler can all find good sport in different settings. Perhaps your triumphs have been on a small pond, with a keep net full of modest sized perch; or perhaps you have gone to a big river and been lucky enough to take a really heavy summer salmon, big enough for you to have it preserved and mounted as a permanent reminder of your good fortune. The modern taxidermist's range of skills and crafts includes an infinite capacity for taking pains, to reproduce accurately the true size and shape and colour of your particular fish in the finished work. And the sight of a fine fish preserved and mounted encourages us all, for it acts as a permanent reminder that there are plenty of other salmon still to be caught, lying waiting in other pools and on other rivers, to provide sport in the days and seasons ahead.

Off-shore, the sea fisherman can make the most of the long days, the fine summer weather and a normally calm sea to anchor on a known mark, perhaps over a sunken wreck or a submerged reef, and fish deep for conger eels, rays and other bottom-living species, and his efforts may be accompanied by the serene cruising and spectacular diving of gannets, streamlined and handsome seabirds which are among the most skilled natural catchers of fish. By comparison, the ubiquitous cormorant has a reptilian and crudely primitive vulturine appearance. Around British coasts one of the most common of all inshore sea fish species is the dogfish, a junior member of the shark family. These and other species fully repay the time and effort expended in gathering and preparing bait. For smaller species this may involve digging in the sands or mud-flats at low tide for lugworms, or dredging with a net for shrimps and myriad other small sea creatures.

If the last of the snow-melt water from the high hills and the recent summer rains in the hills have been reliable, the northern salmon rivers will have begun to attract steady runs of summer salmon and grilse, and by this stage some of the mature cock fish will already be displaying the beginnings of the hooked 'kype' or lower jaw, which denotes a male salmon approaching breeding condition. But if river levels are low the pools may go stale and the first signs of salmon disease may become evident. UDN (ulcerative dermal necrosis) reveals itself by the appearance of ugly patches of fungal infection on the fish's skin, especially around the head and then spreading to the fish's back and flanks in unsightly pallid patches.

As spring gives way to summer on these northern rivers, the salmon fisher may have recourse to a variety of flies. Low water and bright conditions usually indicate that small, dark flies are called for, and patterns like the Stoat's Tail tied on small low water double and treble hooks may take the majority of fish. But a cloudburst in the distant hills or a sudden summer flood may raise and discolour the water considerably, and then it may become necessary to go up significantly in the size of the fly used, and to choose one of the brighter patterns, perhaps quite heavily dressed and mounted on a Waddington-type shank and hook.

The highland river scene is enlivened by the sight and sound of breeding birds. The fluttering flights and distinctive calls of breeding curlews are one of the most characteristic aspects of the uplands in early summer. On the rivers, especially where the flow is swift and bubbling, the dipper is a common sight, bobbing and curtseying as it perches on a boulder and skimming its portly little shape from rock to rock in a blur of wings as it quests for insects and larvae to feed its demanding young.

In the lowlands far to the south the chalk streams in summer present a special challenge for the dry fly fisher, with educated and highly discriminating trout looking askance at any pattern which is not a perfect imitation of their favoured food of the moment. Charms of goldfinches feed on the seed heads of the thistles along the river bank, and on the reservoirs and other stillwaters the best technique is to use a sinking line and a weighted fly or lure to fish deep and slow for the wary rainbow trout of high summer. The trout tend to live chiefly

in the cooler depths of summer stillwaters, or feed at mid-water on the clouds of *Daphnia*, which can be simulated by the mobile, waving fronds of lures dressed with strands of died marabou feathers. On smaller northern lakes the water remains cooler and better oxygenated, and traditional wet fly fishing from a drifting boat is the proven method for success with trout.

In lakes and meres the pursuit of carp calls for determination and dedication through the velvety depths of the short summer nights, while the sea fisher can never be sure of calm waters, even when the quarry is shoals of summer mackerel which swarm to snap at simple feathered lures. The heave and sway of a fishing boat riding at anchor over a mark can be a test for even the stoutest constitution.

By midsummer the brown trout of the richer streams and rivers have ceased to feed with the reckless and undiscriminating abandon of spring. Fly-replete, they have now become highly selective in their choice of food, and the skilfully fished nymph takes the biggest baskets. The fish are in th⌄ very peak of condition, fat and powerful, and the mere act of tightening and setting the hook is enough to galvanise a fish into a frenzied aerial display of jumping and corkscrewing. In rivers and stillwaters the rainbow trout is more susceptible to a well presented sunk fly, nymph or lure when the upper levels of the water are warm and de-oxygenated, for the heat-sensitive brown trout have long ago retired into the deepest and coolest holes.

Finally, summer is the time for the stealthy pursuit of sea trout by night. However low the river may fall, these migratory trout can still run upstream, seemingly able to slip over the stones even when the river is down to a mere trickle. Perhaps the shyest of all game fish, sea trout are wary and elusive by day and seldom move until night has almost come. Then the pools and glides can come alive with the splash and slap of sizeable sea trout on the move.

Abandoning the river in daylight, the dedicated sea trout fisher turns night into day, never wetting his line before the first stars and the first bats have appeared overhead, and fishing steadily through the long and gentle hours of near-twilight until the sun rises again and drives the sea trout back to their deep resting holes during the sunlit daylight hours. The night fisher for sea trout becomes familiar with the other creatures of the dark hours, including the hunting fox, the silent flying owl and the wheeling, aerobatic bats. Himself a predator of sorts, the fisherman finds an affinity with other hunters of the darkness.

AUTUMN

Late summer slides almost imperceptibly into autumn and one of the main indicators of the trout fly fisherman is the gradual disappearance of the last martins and swallows on their southerly migration. The long migration flight to Africa lies ahead, full of challenge and perils, and many do not survive. A fisherman's attention is momentarily distracted by the noisy and agile pursuit of a swallow by a musket or male sparrowhawk, a dashing and deadly chase which ends with the swallow being seized in mid-air by those slender but deceptively powerful talons.

Some of the finest brown trout fishing of the season, both on rivers and lakes, comes in September when the fish feed avidly to store up reserves of energy and condition for the rigours of the coming spawning period. Some of the biggest specimen brown trout fall to a well presented fly — nymph, wet fly or dry fly — in the early autumn. Other species are also making the most of the natural richness of early autumn, and many species of birds feed eagerly on the seeds and berries which abound at this time of year. The first of the migrant snipe arrive in Britain in late September, with large numbers of northern-bred birds swelling the more sedentary populations of British breeding snipe. On the bare stubbles after harvest the partridges suddenly reappear after months of seclusion in the cover of thick hedgerows and standing crops of cereals.

Coarse fishing and the pursuit of grayling both come to the fore in early autumn, when these fish assume prime condition after the debilitating exertions of spring spawning and while there is still ample food for them in the lakes and rivers. Much of the best coarse fishing comes at that special time of year when our summer visiting migrant birds begin to leave these shores and are replaced by wintering migrant geese and duck which have moved south from their northern breeding haunts.

The grayling is pre-eminently an autumn fish, attaining its peak of physical condition with the first frosts and coming readily to a well presented wet fly or a nymph pattern, perhaps a Red Tag or a Sawyer Killer Bug. She may hold the traditional title of 'lady of the stream', but the grayling can make a manfully powerful initial run, and her fighting qualities are enhanced by that large and prominent dorsal fin.

Perch and pike, especially the smaller jack pike, fall readily to spinning lures, and one of the proven and age-old methods of taking these fish in lakes and other still-waters is to fish for them by trolling, with two or three long lines trailing astern as the boat is rowed with steady and practised ease or, more often these days, motoring very slowly while an outboard engine does the work.

Bream favour deep, slow swims in our sluggish rivers and canals, and we fish for these heavy, slab-sided fish in September as the migrant martins and swallows start to leave us, and the first of the new season's duck shooting begins.

The rains of autumn refresh and rejuvenate rivers which may have been low for weeks during the height of summer, and the flood sends an irresistible chemical invitation to those salmon which have been waiting in the estuary for water levels to rise. Now they can run upstream readily, and the urgency of their spawning instincts ensures they lose no time.

In Glen Etive in west Invernesshire the sporting year has reached its peak with the end of the salmon fishing season and the start of the red deer rut. Ptarmigan on the high tops, in their mottled sandy-buff summer plumage, have been in season since 12 August, and the

first parties of wintering geese are beginning to straggle southwards from their northern breeding haunts. The back-end salmon are beginning to display their reddish spawning livery, and the cock fish have the pronounced hooked lower jaw or 'kype' which denotes a male which has come into breeding condition.

On the low ground roebucks and woodcock add to the variety of sporting quarry, and a few brown trout rise readily and feed eagerly on the last insect life before the arrival of the first frosts and the long, cold months of the upland winter. A successful stalking party returns from the hill with a stag on the pony's deer saddle, to find another member of the party in the final stages of playing one of the last salmon of the season.

In the big rivers of the south there are prime barbel, some of the biggest in Britain, to be caught, perhaps by ground baiting a swim with something special like sweet-corn. The match fishing season is now in full swing, each of its participants focusing every ounce of concentration on their stretch of water as they take welcome shelter under their enshrouding umbrellas. Each competitor's world temporarily shrinks as his whole attention is focused on his float. Tense and often fiercely competitive, the day's fishing comes to an end as the final whistle signals it is time to reel in. Then there follows the careful business of weighing-in and the eventual distribution of cash prizes to those with the heaviest keep-nets of fish, and the fish are carefully returned to the water before all the equipment is packed away and the trek back to the cars begins.

Lapwings have formed their winter flocks and clusters of shrieking gulls follow the autumn plough as the tench enthusiasts fish delicately for their quarry. The dedicated carp fisherman slips quietly into position by his chosen mere or pond, to keep a solitary nightlong vigil over his float in hopes of something massive to reward his efforts. His car is parked at a distance, and the first light of day reveals how it has suffered from the unwelcome attentions of a herd of inquisitive cattle.

On all the salmon rivers the season is drawing to a close, and on the larger rivers the boats are prepared for the last few fishing days of the season, often in high water after the first heavy rains of autumn. The cock fish are now heavily marked and each bears the aggressively hooked jaw of the imminent spawner, and on Tweedside the fishing and game shooting seasons overlap, with driven pheasants shot and falling into the river while a flyfisher plays and nets an autumn salmon from a boat. In Norway the last of the season's massive salmon are taken on a ledgered prawn, with the boat giving the angler full command of the river and his fish. Closer to home, Cecilia McPhail catches, prepares and cooks her own salmon before serving it at the table.

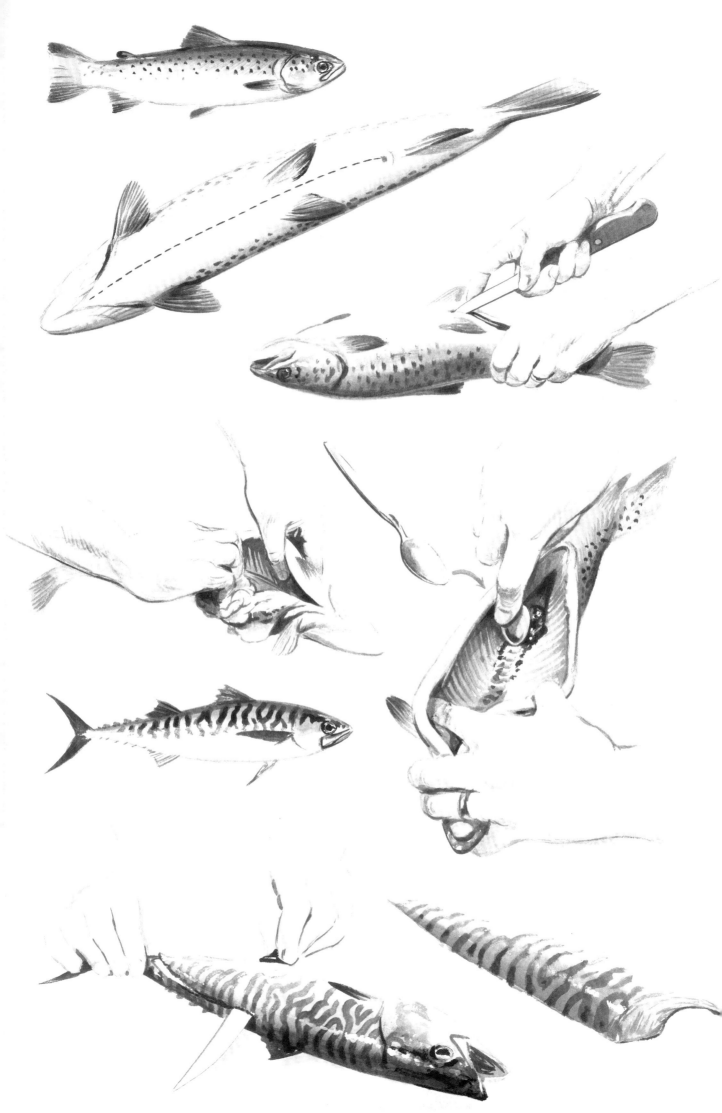

WINTER

Pike are voracious and predatory feeders at all times of the year, but never more so than with the onset of winter. Then they feed with avid appetite to make up the weight and condition they have lost during summer spawning time, and in anticipation of the colder and leaner months which lie ahead. Other species of fish are frequently taken, and trout are a special favourite, but pike will also feed by plucking birds and mammals from the surface of the water. The young of all water birds are at risk, as are the smaller adult birds like the moorhen, and a swimming water vole may be a particularly easy victim. As the days grow shorter the pike comes to its peak of physical condition, and the pike enthusiast has a wide range of plugs, lures and spinners from which to choose.

For all but the dedicated winter grayling fisher the flyfisher's season in Britain is over now, but there is still some enjoyable and absorbing fishing work to be done. Fly boxes must be rearranged and made ready for the coming season. Unreliably rusty hooks must be discarded, and he who likes to tie his own flies can surround himself with the whole panoply of materials from which fishing flies are constructed. Golden pheasant, game cockerel and French partridge each furnish hackle and flank feathers for many well known patterns of salmon and trout flies.

There are small nymphs and long-shanked sea trout lures, tandem flies and small double hooked trout flies, and a range of salmon flies including low water summer patterns tied on single hooks and hairwing flies tied on a Waddington-style shank in a variety of colours and sizes. Feathers from a guineafowl and a turkey also have their places alongside the hair of squirrels — and even a bunch snipped from the coat of the family dog — while a strand of wool from an old jersey is dubbed onto a thread of tying silk and fashioned into a nymph pattern. There is seemingly no end to the enterprising fly-tier's sources of material —

peacocks, pheasants, the wing feathers of a jay and even a few hairs from the head of the artist's son, Gavin McPhail.

As the last anglers leave the water's edge at the close of a successful season, there can sometimes be unhappy reminders of their presence. Carelessly discarded litter clutters the banks and pollution from various sources sullies the waters, a bleak reminder of the fragile vulnerability of all our river systems and inland waters to pollution from industrial, agricultural and domestic sources. Mankind's thoughtlessness and destructive potential are vividly exemplified in the macabre image of a bird's skeleton entangled in the loops of carelessly discarded monofilament line. It is a striking indictment of the abuses which can occur, and a timely reminder that all our sporting fishing and the survival of all our fish species and many types of associated wildlife depend upon the continued purity of our inland and coastal waters.

But with the turn of a page we are suddenly thousands of miles away, in the deep blue waters of the Indian Ocean and confronted with one of the most dramatic and coveted of all big game fish, the blue marlin. Marlin fishing calls for patience, observation and long hours of trolling over known marlin haunts. The specialised big game fishing boats have high-set bridges and high towers from which fish can be spotted at a distance, and in the stern is a swivel seat, the fighting chair from which the angler does battle with his fish once the bait has been taken and the hook securely set.

To be afloat in a smallish craft for many hours on an ocean swell can upset even the most dedicated fisherman, and there is a mixture of agony and ecstasy in doing battle with a big bill-fish while you are also fighting to keep a severe attack of sea sickness at bay. A successful contest means a fine fish in the boat, and the elation of success is mingled with the exhaustion of the long fight and the debilitating misery of sea sickness.

The warm seas of the mid-Atlantic and the Indian ocean present the sea fisherman with a superb variety of especially sporting fish. The sailfish, a cousin of the marlin, is one of the most dramatic and acrobatic of all sporting fish. No sooner does it feel the hook or the resistance of the rod and line than it breaks the surface in a magnificent series of wild,

slashing, head-shaking leaps, almost dancing on its tail in its frenzied efforts to rid itself of the hook. The dorado, or true dolphin, is one of the most distinctively shaped and exquisitely coloured of all fishes. The mature males have a massive domed head, and their flanks are a miracle of subtly iridescent colours, which sadly fade quite quickly after the fish has been caught.

Barracuda are the pike of the high seas, sleek, powerful and opportunistic predators. Their lean and streamlined bodies mean these are fast swimmers, and that pike-like head and jaw contains an array of teeth as formidable as those of any shark. The tuna is neat headed and deeply powerful in the body, shaped for speed and endowed with massive strength and endurance. When hooked near the surface the tuna's instinctive reaction is to plunge for the depths, and the ensuing fight can be prolonged and dogged. It requires strength and stamina to pump a heavy tuna to the surface from a fighting depth of many fathoms.

In Africa the quarry is the massive Nile perch, the river cat-fish and the dashing and aptly named tiger fish, a cousin of the flesh-eating piranha of South America. Formidably equipped with razor sharp teeth and powerful jaws, this is a sporting fish with a speed and power out of all proportion to its size.

Back in Britain, the wintering fieldfares have arrived and the spawning salmon have paired on the redds in the upper reaches of the rivers. A proportion of the fish are caught in specially designed cribs or fish traps. From there the hen fish are gently removed and skilfully stripped of their eggs, and the cock fish's milt is mixed with them to fertilise the reddish-amber beads which will then be transferred to the hatchery. There the eyed ova will be nurtured through the successive stages of alevins, fry and parr, and some will be kept back until they have donned the silvery livery of the smolt, and are ready to be released as migrants into the rivers from which their parents were taken.

The natural activity of spawning involves the excavation of a shallow depression or redd in the river gravel by the female using vigorous and sinuous body movements to wash the gravel away. Then the eggs are shed into the redd and the attendant male sheds his milt directly over them. The rigours of spawning cause high mortality among salmon, and it is not uncommon to find dead and dying fish along the upper reaches of salmon rivers in the winter months.

Winter is prime fishing time for many coarse fishers, and ledgered baits can take good baskets of fish from carefully chosen swims. The landscape by the river is bare and stark, the trees stripped of all the rich foliage of summer by the winds and frosts of autumn and winter. On northern rivers the grayling is a favourite winter fish, and the traditional recipe for success is to trot a gilt-tailed worm on light tackle downstream, the dipping of the tiny float indicating a bite. Winter grayling are in the very peak of condition and exhibit sporting qualities quite different from their sluggish summer behaviour.

And so we come to the end of Rodger McPhail's artistic odyssey through the fisherman's year. It is time for reflection and relaxation, perhaps with a good book and in the comfort of your favourite armchair, for fishing is blessed with a wonderfully rich and varied literature. Although Isaak Walton was not the first angling writer, his *Compleat Angler* has a unique place in the early literature of the sport. The garb and the tackle have changed and evolved in many ways since Walton's day, and even since the golden age of Victorian fisherman like Halford, but the quiet pleasures and satisfactions of sporting fishing remain undiminished by the passing of many generations.